WHERE

on

EARTH?

EUROPE

By Shalini Vallepur

Designed by Brandon Mattless

Photo Credits

Words that look like **this** can be found in the glossary on page 24.

BookLife PUBLISHING

©2020
BookLife Publishing Ltd.
King's Lynn
Norfolk PE30 4LS

ISBN: 978-1-83927-053-6

Written by:
Shalini Vallepur

Edited by:
William Anthony

Designed by:
Brandon Mattless

CONTENTS

WHAT IS A CONTINENT?

A continent is a large area of land. There are seven continents on Earth. The continents are surrounded by five oceans.

North America

Arctic Ocean

Europe

Asia

Atlantic Ocean

South America

Pacific Ocean

Africa

Indian Ocean

Antarctica

Australia

Southern Ocean

N
W
E
S

The **population** of Earth lives on the seven continents. Each continent has different types of weather and **landscape**, as well as different **cultures** and ways of living.

Let's learn about Europe!

WELCOME TO EUROPE!

Where on Earth is Europe? Europe is a continent that is north of Africa and to the west of Asia.

Eiffel Tower in Paris, France

Colosseum in Rome, Italy

The population of Europe is well over 700 million.

There are 50 countries in Europe. For some countries, only a part of them is in Europe. For example, the eastern part of Russia is in Asia.

St Basil's Cathedral in Moscow, Russia

LANGUAGES

Around 150 languages are spoken in Europe. Many Europeans are **bilingual**. This means they can speak and understand more than one language.

Let's learn how to say 'hello' in some European languages!

ZDRAVSTVUJTYE
RUSSIAN

HYVÄÄ PÄIVÄÄ
FINNISH

HOLA
SPANISH

GUTEN TAG
GERMAN

HELLO
ENGLISH

YASOU
GREEK

How many languages can you speak?

EUROPEAN WEATHER

The Equator runs through the middle of the Earth. Places that are closer to the Equator are warmer than places that are farther away.

Europe is north of the Equator and is in the Northern Hemisphere.

Equator

The **climate** across Europe is very different. There are four seasons in Europe; winter, spring, summer and autumn. It gets colder in winter and warmer in summer.

Snowy Finland

Sunny Italy

Winters in Finland and Italy are different because Italy is closer to the Equator.

Fact File:
UNITED KINGDOM

The United Kingdom is made up of four countries. England, Scotland and Wales are on one island, and Northern Ireland is on another.

Scotland

Edinburgh

Northern Ireland

Belfast

England

Wales

London

Cardiff

Atlantic Ocean

There are lots of different types of landscape in the United Kingdom. There are beaches and cliffs around the **coast**. People walk and cycle in forests.

Cliffs in Caister-on-Sea

Forest in England

Fact File:

Population:
Over 60 million people

Biggest city:
London
(over 8 million people)

Tallest mountain:
Ben Nevis
(1,345 metres)

EUROPEAN ANIMALS

There are many **species** of animal in Europe. Many of them are **adapted** to live there.

Reindeer are found in the cold northern countries of Norway, Sweden, Finland, Greenland and Russia. Their thick coats of fur keep them warm.

Bacgers can be found all over Europe. They have sharp claws to help them dig **burrows**.

Badger in a burrow

Fact File:
GREECE

Greece

Greece is in southeast Europe. Summers in Greece are very hot. Greece is one of the closest European countries to the Equator. Lots of people visit Greece to enjoy the hot weather.

Athens

Greece has thousands of islands. How many can you count?

Greek city

Many people live in cities. Some people live in villages and towns in the countryside.

Greek village

Fact File:

Population:
Around 11 million

Biggest city:
Athens (around 3 million people)

Tallest mountain:
Mount Olympus (2,917 metres)

PLANTS and TREES

Pine trees are adapted to grow in cold areas of Europe. Their trunks are covered in thick **bark**. This protects them against the cold.

Pine trees

Many flowers bloom in spring and summer when it is warmer and sunnier.

Tulips bloom in the Netherlands during spring.

Lavender and sunflowers bloom in France during summer.

Fact File:
ROMANIA

Romania is in eastern Europe. Romania's landscape has lots of mountains, hills and **plains**.

Romania

Bucharest

Black Sea

Most people live in cities, but some people live in **medieval** towns. Many people travel to Romania to visit the medieval towns.

Bucharest

Medieval town

Fact File:

Population:
Around 19 million

Biggest city:
Bucharest (around 2 million people)

Tallest mountain:
Moldoveanu (2,544 metres)

EUROPEAN FOOD

There are millions of people in Europe and everyone has to eat! Let's look at some tasty food from Europe.

Borscht is a bright-red beet soup from eastern Europe.

Bratwurst is a type of sausage from Germany.

Waffles from Belgium are often served with fruit and chocolate.

Bukta is a sweet bread filled with jam that comes from Hungary.

GLOSSARY

adapted	changed over time to suit the environment
bark	the hard outside of a tree trunk
bilingual	being able to speak two languages very well
burrows	holes or tunnels dug by an animal
climate	the common weather in a certain place
coast	the area of land next to the ocean
cultures	the traditions, ideas and ways of life of groups of people
landscape	how the land is laid out
medieval	something that is from around AD 500 to AD 1500 in Europe
plains	large areas of flat land with a few trees
population	the number of people living in a certain area, such as a city or country
species	a group of very similar animals or plants that can create young together

INDEX